A Nonsense Rhyme

The Sing-Sing Song of the Flapper-Jacker-Whacker-O

Tales from The Whimple Wood
Volume III

Written by John F. Smith
Edited by Odette E. Colón and Susan Hayden
Illustrated by Odette E. Colón

Published by
CHINKY-PO TREE, INC.
Atlanta, Georgia

First Edition

Library of Congress Catalog Card Number: 95-67455
ISBN 1-884375-02-2

Published by Chinky-Po Tree, Inc.
Printed in the USA

To Sue Pritchett,
My
Buddha-Bear,
who gently, gently
beckons me on my path—
to love, to laugh, to live at last.

The Sun laughs, the Moon smiles and the Stars wink daily over a special place called The Whimple Wood. Inside these pages you will meet another resident of The Whimple Wood, the Flapper-Jacker-Whacker-O. "The Flapper", for short, is full of energy and spends his day playing, playing, playing! Sometimes he is naughty but mostly he is just who he is. We hope you enjoy him.

I am

the

Flapper-

Jacker-

Whacker-

O!

And I whittle and I hacker
With my two-penny hatchet
On a chinky-poly stump;

And I thump, thump, thump
On a bump, bump, bump
With my two-penny hatchet
On a chinky-poly stump.

And I flutter and I stutter
While I piddle and I putter
With my periwinkle supper
On a periwinkle rock;

And I rattle and I prattle
Like a loon a-drivin' cattle,
Or a drummer in the band
Going rata-tata-tat.

And I munch, munch, munch
On my lunch, lunch, lunch
At my periwinkle supper
On the periwinkle rock.

And when my supper's over
Well, I scuttle to the clover
Where I chase the bouncing bunnies
To their roly-poly holes;

How they clatter and they scatter
When my feet begin to patter
As I chase the bouncing bunnies
To their roly-poly holes.

Then I rap, rap, rap
And I tap, tap, tap
At the roly-poly entrance
Where the bunnies disappear;

But inspite of all my rapping
And my gentle tippy-tapping
With my heart a-flippy-flapping
Not a bunny reappears!

Then I go among the corn
Feeling awfully forlorn
At my silly-nilly efforts
When the buns were hoppin 'round,

For it's no fun-funny
For to chase a bouncing bunny
When he settles down to runny
To his holey in the ground.

In the corn I go a-jumpin'
Till I find a yellow punkin,
And I settle down to thumpin'
On the yellow punkin rind;

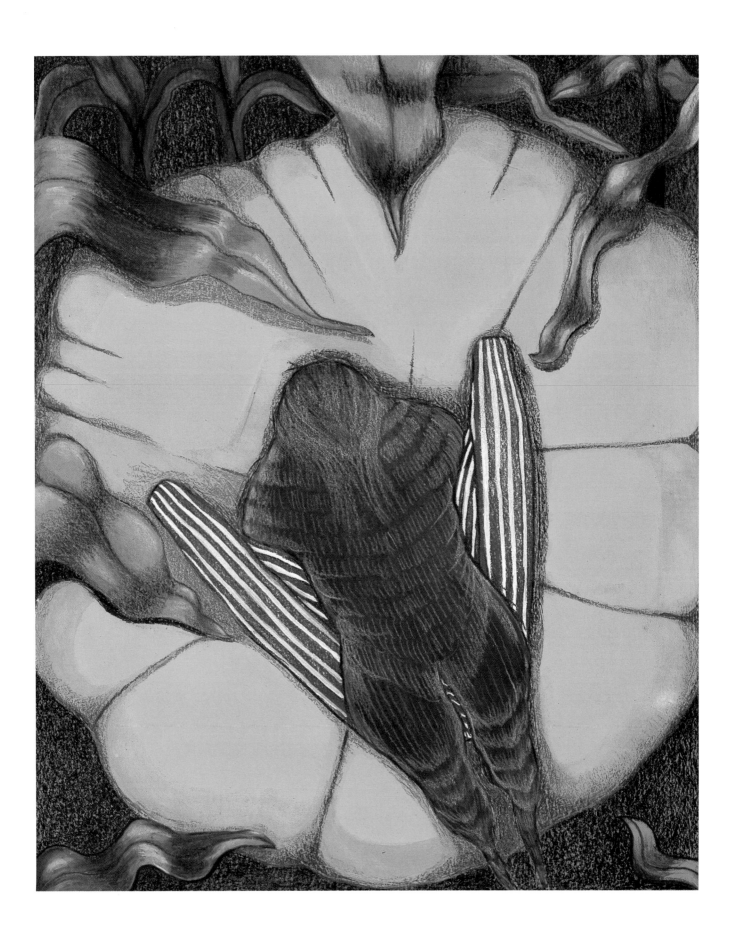

And I pick, pick, pick
With a chinky-poly stick,
Turning feathers into ruffles
With my scuffles and my shuffles.

And the pennies that I find
Are made of yellow punkin rind,
And they roll among the pebbles
Like a flock of little rebels!

Yes, I keep thump, thump, thumpin'
On a punk, punk, punkin'
With a rata-tata-tat
Of a drummer drum-drummin';

And I stagger and I hobble,
And I swagger and I bobble,
And I wiggle and I run
Like a belly full of fun!

But when my eyes are dreamy
And the night is growing squeamy,
I scuttle to my holey
In the chinky-poly tree;

Where I sleep, sleep, sleep
Without a peep, peep, peep
In my holey where I'm dreamin'
In the chinky-poly tree.

'Till the sunny-sun-sun
With a twinkle and a run
Comes a-climbin' up the heavens
Telling folks the night is done!

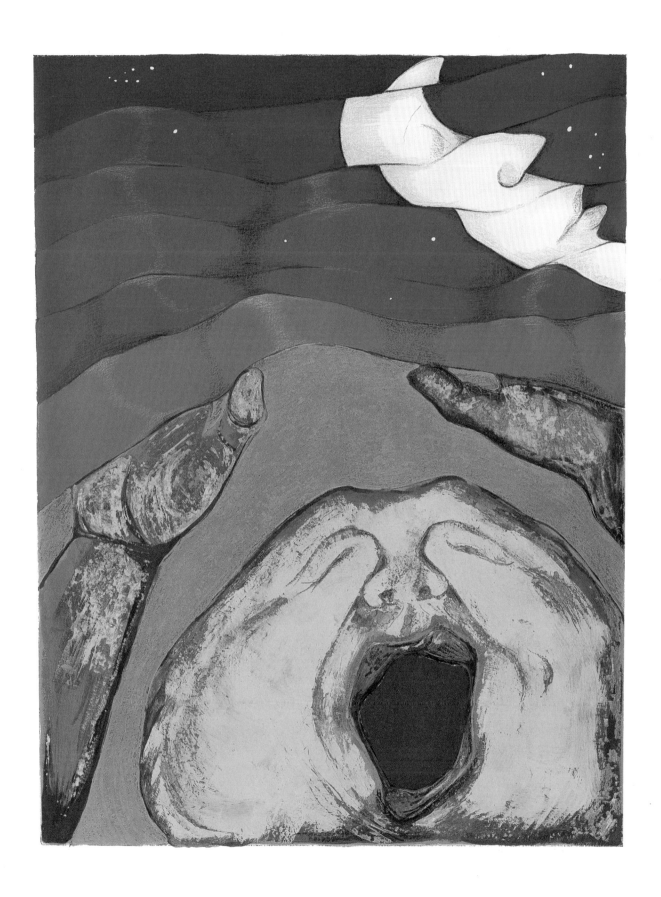

Night-Night

XOX

"The Flapper"

Publishers Statement

A Nonsense Rhyme, The Sing-Sing Song of the Flapper-Jacker-Whacker-O, the third volume of *Tales From The Whimple Wood* introduces readers to yet another of John F. Smith's delightful characters. The Flapper-Jacker-Whacker-O, overly energetic and refreshingly silly, fills his days in The Whimple Wood in the pursuit of fun and activity. His relentless motion shapes him as a mischievous character who desires interaction with the other critters that share his world. He endears himself to readers through his exaggerated antics.

The Flapper-Jacker-Whacker-O joins the Wapiti-Hoo and the Whango-Whee in a series of books that depict the lives of the inhabitants of The Whimple Wood, a safe and magical place that invites readers of all ages to enter and celebrate. It is with great pleasure that we present you with another fine book in our continuing collection.

Chinky-Po Tree, Inc.

John F. Smith

About the Author

John Franklin Smith was a renowned scholar of his day, a true Renaissance man. Born in Fayetteville, Tennessee in 1877, he joined the faculty of Berea Academy, a part of Berea College in Kentucky in 1911. For the 20 years he was at this institution, Smith's primary teaching responsibilities were in the area of rural social science. However, during most of his adult life, he pursued special lines of study, with each year being devoted to a particular field. Among the many subjects Smith covered were mythology and folklore, forestry, animal life, botany, history, criminology, child welfare, race relations, English and American literature, balladry, and children's literature.

As a citizen he was involved in a variety of areas of public service, among which were Kentucky's Interracial Commission, Kentucky's Children's Code Commission, and the Kentucky Child Welfare Commission. Following his love of language, Smith was one of the early editors of *Kentucky Folk-lore and Poetry Magazine.*

A great outdoorsman, many of Smith's interests and his great love of nature came together in the poems he wrote and the pictures he drew for his own two children, Frank and James. Although Smith died in 1940, his love of nature and literature and his own creativity continues in the characters and their lives in *The Whimple Wood,* the imaginary place Smith created through poetry and art for his sons. This book is an artist's interpretation of Smith's original poem. This and the other books in this series, *Tales From The Whimple Wood,* introduce today's child to Smith's legacy and a whole world of creativity.

About the Illustrator

Odette E. Colón was born in Old San Juan, Puerto Rico, and was raised
and educated in Europe and the United States. She studied fine arts at
Virginia Commonwealth University and The University of Georgia.
A great lover and collector of children's books, Odette has fulfilled a
lifelong dream in the recent founding of Chinky-Po Tree, Inc. This is
her second children's book.

A Page of Thanks

Thanks to Cappie Harper whose unfaltering love and enthusiasm inspires me on good days and bolsters me on bad ones. To Nancy Hull whose critical eye and playful spirit provided a great sounding board. To Nancy Blaschke for listening carefully and teaching me more than she'll ever know. To Sherry Thacker for enjoying the same silly things and whose keen perception made an essential difference. To Susan Hayden for her generous editorial contribution. And last but not least, to "Joeyhead" Hannaford who provides a mysterious but essential ingredient in the CPT, Inc. trio and whose technical back-up makes all our work tangible instead of ethereal.

More of the
Tales From The Whimple Wood
Series...

The Song of the Whango-Whee
Tales From The Whimple Wood Volume I
by John F. Smith
Illustrated by Odette E. Colón
Handlettering by Joey Hannaford

The Whango-Whee is an enchanting bird-like creature who wears a cloak of
soft purplish feathers. He lives *"high up in the chinky-po tree"* where he *"sings
to the dreamy moon/ and the stars in the milky way"* and of his life deep in
The Whimple Wood. The Whimple Wood is filled with creatures whose wacky antics
will at the same time stimulate children's imaginations and woo them to sleep.
This is an engaging adventure for parent,
grandparent and child alike.

The Wapiti-Hoo
Tales From The Whimple Wood Volume II
by John F. Smith
Illustrated by Joey Hannaford

This second installment from the *Tales From The Whimple Wood* series features the
fantasmical Wapiti-Hoo. The Wapiti-Hoo never quite knows where life will lead him.
He is an adventurous fellow who is always looking for a companion to share in his
exploits. In this delighfully fanciful book, the Wapiti-Hoo befriends a child and
together they share in the enchantment of the sea and outer space, returning back home
to the comforts of the sleepy-time world.. This book incorporates playful fun,
imaginative word-play and rich imagery to help
ease youngsters into a pleasant sleep.

Songs of The Whimple Wood
Volume I
by Songwriter/Producer Louisa Branscomb

Children cannot be still when listening to this collection of songs by award-winning
songwriter Louisa Branscomb. This audio cassette tape features lullabies, sing-alongs, and
dance tunes about the various creatures of The Whimple Wood. Some songs were
created to be interactive, with the liner notes containing movements for children to act
out with the music. A great companion for family trips in the car and the perfect
complement to the books of the *Tales From The Whimple Wood* series. Available in
bookstores, gift and record stores in the Spring of 1995.

Song of the Flapper-Jacker-Whacker-O

Words and Music by Louisa Branscomb

I'm the Flapper-Jacker-Whacker
And I whittle and I hacker
With my two penny hatchet
On the chinky-po stump.
(thump, thump, bump-bump-bump)
Yes I whittle and I hacker
With a ticky-ticky tacker
With a rappin' and a tappin'
And a bump bump bump!
(Thump, thump, bump-bump-bump)

(Chorus)
I love to go a funnin'
Underneath the sun 'n
Just a-jumpin and a-bumpin' till the day is done.
(Jump, jump, bump-bump-bump)

And...then...I
Like to go a runnin'
Just a-playin and a-funnin'
And a chasin' all the bun's in-
To their roly poly holes.
(Rap, rap, tap-tap-tap)
But it's no fun-funny
When I cannot find a bunny
And I get sort of lonely
And down a-goes the sun.
(Down, down, down goes the sun!)

(Chorus)

And...then...I...
Go a bump-bumpin'
And a-thumpin on a punkin'
Plunkin' and a plunkin'
Like a military drum.
(Rat, tat, rat-tat-tat)

And I stagger and I hobble
And I swagger and I bobble
And I wiggle and I wobble
Like a belly full of fun.
(Fun, fun, fun-fun-fun!)

(Following to tune of chorus;)

I love to go a funnin'
Underneath the sun
And jumpin and a-bumpin' till the day is done.
But my eyes are gettin' dreamy
The night is gettin' squeamy
I think I'll go a sleepin'
Till the night is done.
(*Whisper:* Sleep, sleep, not a peep!)

Yes, I'm the...
Flapper-Jacker-Whacker
And I whittle and I hacker
With my two penny hatchet
On the chinky-po stump.
(Thump, thump, bump-bump-bump)
And I stagger and I hobble
And I swagger and I bobble
And I think I better wobble
To my chinky-po tree.
(Thump, thump, bump-bump-bump)

Song of the Flapper-Jacker-Whacker-O
is featured on the audio cassette
*Songs of The Whimple Wood,
Volume I*
written and produced by Louisa Branscomb
for Chinky-Po Tree, Inc.